New York Poems

Also by D. H. Melhem

Poetry

NOTES ON 94TH STREET

REST IN LOVE

CHILDREN OF THE HOUSE AFIRE / More Notes on 94th Street

COUNTRY: An Organic Poem

POEMS FOR YOU (chapbook)

CONVERSATION WITH A STONEMASON

Prose

BLIGHT: A Novel

HEROISM IN THE NEW BLACK POETRY:
Introductions and Interviews

GWENDOLYN BROOKS: Poetry and the Heroic Voice

REACHING EXERCISES: The IWWG Workshop Book

Editor

MOSAIC: Poems from an IWWG Workshop

A DIFFERENT PATH: An Anthology of RAWI (co-editor Leila Diab)

Musical Drama

CHILDREN OF THE HOUSE AFIRE

D. H. MELHEM

New York Poems

NOTES ON 94TH STREET

CHILDREN OF THE HOUSE AFIRE/
More Notes on 94th Street

SYRACUSE UNIVERSITY PRESS

Syracuse University Press
Syracuse, New York 13244-5160

First Edition 2005
05   06   07   08   09   10   6   5   4   3   2   1

New York Poems combines two separate titles:

Notes on 94th Street, copyright © 1972 by D. H. Melhem. The Poet's Press, New York, 1972. Second edition copyright © 1979 by D. H. Melhem. Dovetail Press, New York, 1979. Library of Congress Catalog Card Number: 79-50706. Second edition contains revisions and additional poems.

Children of the House Afire / More Notes on 94th Street. Copyright © 1976 by D. H. Melhem. Dovetail Press, New York, 1976. Library of Congress Catalog Card Number: 76-559-50. "Broadway Music" originally introduced this book and also opens the second edition of *Notes on 94th Street.*

Several poems from both works are newly revised.

"Requiescant 9/11" is the closing section of *Conversation with a Stonemason.* Copyright © 2003 by D. H. Melhem. IKON, New York, 2003.

"Prospect" was originally inspired by the Angel Project, New York's Lincoln Center Festival, 2003. Its epigraph, comprising verses from the Second and Ninth *Duino Elegies* by Rainer Maria Rilke, translated by C. F. MacIntyre, appear in his version, © 1961 by C. F. MacIntyre, University of California Press, fourth printing, Berkeley and Los Angeles, 1968. To all, grateful acknowledgment is made.

My deepest appreciation goes to Mary Selden Evans for her steadfast support of this project, to Kassy Wilson for bringing the manuscript to her attention, to Kathleen Benson, especially, and also to Bob Shamis and Melanie Bower of the Museum of the City of New York for their assistance, to Laraine Goodman and Hayan Charara for help when it was needed, and to Dana Vogel, Gregory M. Vogel, and George Meyer for their sustaining faith.

Library of Congress Cataloging-in-Publication Data

Melhem, D. H.
  [Notes on 94th Street]
  New York poems / D.H. Melhem.— 1st ed.
    p. cm.
  ISBN 0-8156-0813-6 (alk. paper)
  1. New York (N.Y.)—Poetry. I. Melhem, D. H. Children of the house afire. II. Title.
PS3563.E442N6 2005
811'.54—dc22   2005013480

Manufactured in the United States of America

To the City of New York
embattled, gallant, enduring

Contents

loving

perspectives

heroines and heroes

CHILDREN OF THE HOUSE AFIRE/
More Notes on 94th Street   89

Preface

"Olde New York" with its horse-drawn carriages traversing Central Park and its "Great White Way" of Broadway theaters . . . the Empire City with its invincible skyline . . . these idealized images seem to have ended abruptly on September 11, 2001. Lower Broadway, with viewing platform facing Ground Zero's sixteen acres of devastation, became the street's main attraction. Yet each year and decade has shaken with its own turbulence. The 1970s, for example, were not halcyon days for the City. Nor were they, on a personal level, for me.

My beloved mother had died in 1969. As an only child overcome with grief, I tried to write her an elegy. The task was too painful. *Rest in Love*, a book of poems, would take more than five years to complete. Meanwhile, I turned to my immediate surroundings. I sat by my second-floor window on 94th Street and observed the chaos and change that seemed to mirror my own life. The street became my Muse.

As the daughter of Lebanese immigrants and a native of Brooklyn, New York, I always felt myself to be quintessentially American. I grew up learning to appreciate people of all backgrounds in my neighborhood (a Protestant among Irish and Italian Catholics, a Gentile among Jews) and within my own family. My maternal aunts and uncles had married people as diverse as an aristocratic Englishman, a Belgian-French wine merchant, an Irish nurse, and a German house painter. Although I was taken with the West Side's natural beauty (the Hudson River, Riverside and Central Parks) and its astringent intellectual, artistic, and political atmosphere, my family's eclecticism drew me to the area's abundant and ever-renewing human tableaux.

In 1950, I married a prospective teacher, whose Greek and Russian immigrant parents had settled in the Bronx and then in Pelham, New York. Chester and I moved midway between the families into Manhattan, where we resided in a White, middle class enclave on the Upper West Side, surrounded by poor Puerto Rican, Black, and White neighbors. Some of them were crowded into SROs (Single Room Occupancy, city-supported hotels). We also lived with whores, pimps, and crazies who were being dumped out of overcrowded mental institutions into the streets, along with angry, sometimes neglected children who occasionally preyed on others for money. Our daughter and son attended public schools, where they made friends and tried to avoid dangerous encounters.

During this time, Urban Renewal, chastised as "Negro Removal," was busily tearing down old buildings, erecting low-income housing projects, and supporting private renovation of old brownstones. Parents battled over school redistricting, busing, and other well-intentioned programs to integrate schools. Many middle-class parents fled to the suburbs, leaving their friends behind.

Throughout its roiling transitions, my husband and I remained devoted to our neighborhood. By the 1980s, a building boom and rampant gentrification hastened the disappearance of "Mom and Pop" stores, neighborhood bookshops, and the leveling of many unprotected landmarks. Spacious Art Deco movie houses, like the Riverside, the Riviera, and the New Yorker, gave way to shiny new supermarkets and high-rise apartments. The Symphony Theater, now Symphony Space, a performing arts center encased within a large, upscale residential building, is the sole survivor among the local movie palaces.

The West Side continues to attract ethnic groups—Asians, especially Koreans, Indians, and Pakistanis, and more recently Africans, from all areas. The newest language on the block is an ancient one: Arabic, in several dialects.

And so I welcome you to my neighborhood. While these poems witness another era, they celebrate the dynamics of urban change, the raucous vitality of this great City.

D. H. M.

NOTES ON 94TH STREET

In extreme times, character becomes

the rarest expression of genius.

We move among heroines and heroes

whose impulse to liberty and social justice

persists as dragon's teeth.

Foreword

D. H. Melhem's work has the kind of tough grittiness that sustains the reader with the hope of wonder. For wonder at the variety of life, at the ability to keep going on, is a kind of hope. If one wonders at the human will not only to survive but to create a flower out of the bread of woe, then one believes—and hopes— the next step, and the step after that, and finally almost the most impossible mountains are capable of being scaled.

But her hope is not facile, nor sustained with sentimental panaceas of verbal brotherhood. It is tough and stubbornly rooted in the observance of the world before her. The style with which she presents her world is spare and brilliantly hard. A world of enormous feeling animates her work, but it is contained within the style of craftsman-technician, and controlled by the scalpel of a poet.

The world she describes is not a pretty one, but it is a world swirling with passion, obsession and divine madness. Once she has introduced the reader to it, its power and its force inevitably, deeply overwhelm him.

Martin Tucker, Editor
Confrontation

Introduction

A notable beauty and virtue of D. H. Melhem's poetry is that, with a fully articulated sense of her own location . . . the ability to set out her hearth anywhere . . . she keeps a warm and open alertness to other landscapes, most especially, here, that of 94th Street, past Broadway. She knows very well that a poet can do himself and his readers the most serious disservice in pretending to a nativity which is not his. D. H. Melhem entertains a warm and eloquent identification with the sidewalk and apartment life of 94th Street. She can speak with the voice of a Panther, of an upper-class lady, a whole succession of walkers and gleaners and bystanders. Her adoption of voices, her response to her neighborhood terrain, is a reaching gesture: that gesture of grace which any really good poet, or writer, knows is a needful grace for her or his writing, an all-essential gesture of generosity and candor. D. H. Melhem, like an encouragingly enlarging number of American poets, apprehends the virtue and beauty of coming as an outsider to the lands beyond one's hearthside; embracing neither the rash and false-humble superstition that other people's experience is essentially "inaccessible," (hence, not to be written about); nor, yet, the egomaniac fallacy that one's own little ego-capital is a bottomless pond. D. H. Melhem, like others of her generation, is bringing poetry back to a vigorous, beauteous and too-long-in-these-quarters discarded function: a tool of inquiry and correspondence and clear, true-functioning response. I am honored and excited to present her work.

Donald Phelps

for dana and gregory
who grow here

and my beloved west side

Broadway Music

The musicians at the newsstand
are singing
they sing and play instruments
the saxophone and cracked guitar
bawl and whine over exhaust fumes and garbage dust
they play and play   the dirty black cap open between them
on the ground —
two old men for pennies.

And a big, drunken woman laughs
laughs over her balloon stomach
she pulls up her sweater to show it
the string holding up her skirt
hanging from the big white belly
she laughs through the spaces between her teeth
her mouth looks purple and half-vacant
                    when she opens it
she shows the old men her distended belly
as if it were fruitful or cherished
she lifts her paper bag to her mouth
like a trumpet — and drinks.

She is singing now, softly, then begins
a hard hoarse cry of a note
and holds it. She is singing —
a little wine left in the bottle
the flavor that was in it
a harsh joy in the emptying

And the old men sing with her
they dream through the curving wood and metal
and the forms of the sounds that go out
as if the dirty newspapers and today's news
the people running up subway stairs
the dogs the pimps the hustlers the
gleaning-eyed girls, the howling police cars
their bullhorn commands, the litter
and dust-filtered daylight
as if these held the moment of art
as if it could be made
from the unlovely flesh, half-clay, half-dust
as if it could all be molded again, and the players
were gods empowering a new music

the big-bellied woman
and the musicians
at the newsstand

Tough Babe doesn't beg

Tough Babe doesn't beg
she says, gimme.
Gimme a quarter, gimme a dime,
gimme.   Demands her due,
asserts
her worth to the street.

No please. It isn't a favor.
You're not absolved by giving.
Something in your pocket
belongs to her,
she believes.

This tourist, resident

This tourist, resident
cruises Broadway's exotic islands,
sees
toilet paper in the trees
where
bench to bench
communities oppose
their rows of misery
cross street.

Old men together
face the sun
resting
arthritic argument against the past.
Sleeping it off
drunks and junkies sprawl
cynicism, defeat
in beer cans,
suck dreams from paper bags.

horse at the corner

in dirty pockets
dollars brokenfaced
with change
collect for passage
glassine bags
packed for trips that round
will end at the corner
emptying on faces having taken
no joy from joy
but the pursuit
catches them like cops

little crowd
flings outward
shooting burnout stars

on 94th street

on 94th Street
rain upon snow the long summer long
where footsteps tire and tireless the track
of wheels and window-washing
over cracks that rattle carts
and carriages of babies flying down
a hill of stillness shouted into dark
to everyone who hurrying along will
shuffle back no ending starts and
stirs again alarming moans and
calling out of tune will ruin
silences the sweep of sun one touch
is touching one is touching it
a friend of evening
with you

Dogbaby

Lady buying carrots and two pears:
that is a dogbaby in your carriage.

It's warm.
You've tucked the blanket anyway
around his collar (hers).
Confusion
of identity. I mean
precisely who or what
or where one takes the proper space
among his peers.

Is it a dog?
A baby?

Or having done with categories
are dogs and babies
all the same to you?

(song)

Lady, that is a dogbaby in your carriage
Lady, that is a dogbaby in your carriage
Lady, that is a dogbaby in your carriage
it's warm
you've tucked the blanket anyway
buying your carrots
today

picketing jimmy's

they're picketing jimmy's
the fruit and vegetable store
california grapemounds
picked by scabs

jimmy fights back
his radio
flings news and music
pellets of static

marty and irwin cry
don't buy
don't break the strike
chavez   grapepickers   four years
bunching grief
into union

jimmy says
I am a working man
and make an honest living
on his radio
a group sings love
the news is all disaster
jimmy lifts a bunch of grapes
messages from california
he won't receive

supermarket

mister manager, last week
this little can of peas was twenty cents
today it's two for forty-five
think I think that's cheaper?

boy opens carton stamps cantops
new price you call smiling to distract me
over cartful of
chickenbacks soupbones and canned beans
things I can afford
not what I like

mister manager, this marketing
grows bitter
meatless dinners now
and fishless
we'll be eating grits and gruel
before you're through
shall I blame the system only
are you wicked, too?

Order Boy

You grow old,
order boy,
will not be
manager,
or own much.
You grow sideburns
marking a style,
eyes recede
fearing traffic,
the truth of revolving
in place.

I see your years
that yearn to
get off your bicycle
overturning
burdens carefully boxed
as you pedal to apartments
and return,
same pace.

A Pisser*

That's right: adjust your hat.
The main thing is
your hat on straight.

You make
a statement.
I recognize
revolt
as I see
your head
erect
over your cane
and crouching thighs
that spit
profanities
in the street,
nearly home.

*title courtesy of Paul Blackburn

P I Z Z A

we're here, after the movie
for a ritual slice
with sodawine, stand
in a light without grace
at the formica counter

pizzaman
toss high in silence the pizzadoughball
that falls flat on your fist
whirling it wider
how lean the thinning disc can leap and spin
don't break it
on the clench that curves your arm to wait
and spring
and wait

have mercy on
the form rejected flung and wound
too many times
before it yields in one irreversible winding
an incorrigible
gap

smiley's deli

pale face congealing over
eyeslits
thin cut making
a mouth
pallor of hands
extends
the round steel blade
slicing up roast beef
becomes a scale precise to
fractions of fractions
of a pound
slivered pastrami
never handcut
the old way

smiley's assistant
hates him
puts extra meat
in sandwiches
another piece of pickle
when he's not looking

customers
come in
gaze at price lists
and pay

truckman has
beer and bologna on roll
sits at the table for one
end of the counter

two schoolboys want franks
complain about
meager sauerkraut
smiley takes
a dollar from
the beggar lifting his eyepatch
to examine
corned beef with cole slaw on rye

watching the counter window
where pickles go
and macaroni salad
and orange lox
sliced fine as crepe de chine
we eat

Lore, at Green's

Lore crochets
a string necklace,
steadies
a fur headband
with grosgrain,
replaces
with shoelace
boot zipper,
finds that
most things
can be salvaged.

Mr. Lee's Laundry

handpress
the hours
into tickets
that season
your children
at school
pack sheets
and shirts
like bundles
of books
cleanly
stacked
to be
opened

Dogwalker

Poodles are pretty,
clipped.
Mine's friendly.
We walk
where riverside trees
cherry blossom,
boats meet briefly,
dogs encounter,
nice people sun themselves
dressed up.

This neighborhood
was tiptop:
streets were clean.
Now:
doors doublelocked,

the poor
everywhere.

unnaturals

he and he and
she and she walk
hand in hand

we rebuke them
(me and me)

accident

crossing the street, he glanced left
saw death his mother sitting in a truck
bore down on him
smashed face that flew forth
twenty feet to rest   red in the eyes
light streaming from his brain
      C A L L   T H E   P O L I C E
police are questioning   their questions
      lying around the man

a lady gives a handkerchief

long after bearer and the stretcherborne
facts like ghosts
harrow their ground
translate a man
to measurement
from bumper to blood puddle
equate the rate with
mass and distance of him

truth cools to mathematics
intern of the ambulance
records
the patient waited thirty minutes
bled to death

Crier   (song)

Crier
wears a hat with three roses
hands hang empty the length of her coat

over timid shuffling
her body dips and droops
                    Nobody laughs
who passes
                her crooked hat
her eyes that glitter tears
upon the dark
                    as she
cries up 94th Street
every night

by the hudson

I see the gray gull
above him an eagle I cannot see
limns brilliant passage
gull hovers   hopes fish   but
I am watching the sky behind him
wing distances dust me with light
the wind lives

Slum Garbage Collection

It isn't better
I promise
it will not be.
If you, indeed,
derive your night from hell
then howl, Joe Corepus, on the curb,
and be content.
For we collect your refuse frequently
before elections.
Wrecked cars and derelicts
are litter
we clear away, sometimes.
Consider your garbage bags: corpse-like they
rot together and revive
as beetles, roaches, rats.
Sit on the stoop, Joe. There you grow
rigid. No matter,
that's the spirit.
Wasn't it
one everlasting stench,
your putrefying bananas, condoms, brains,
pain in all cavities,
a creeping pyorrhea of the will I still can smell, here
above garbage spilling your death upward
into my nose hairs?

From the Second Floor

The second floor is colloquy.
My room extends the street.
I can call down to quiet,
answer police,
alarm, rebuke all anguish
and all singing
at inappropriate times.

The second floor
is sociologist, reports
at 4:00 a.m.
sodomy between parked cars.
Dogs defecate
upon the news lying
in lumps that pustulate
the street. A scream
evaporates. Cars
carry music to the water.

From the second floor
the river sounds
to the left.

From the Sixteenth Floor

Glass between us is thin
collecting cloud
upon surface.
Cold outside, inside
the steam heats.
Positions distinct:
there complaint,
spittled cries rising
against
impassive windows closed.
We have defenses:

storm panes, conditioners
lock our air in height
above all common practice
of defeat.
From the sixteenth floor one takes
a middle space.
Figure in the street, right,
is visual.

Musicale

Next door they are playing Mendelssohn.
Well, I think it's Mendelssohn.
It would be nice to knock
and ask.
I imagine calling
through the wall,
"Mendelssohn?"

Piano, cello, and a violin:
my neighbor, Mrs. G., two of her friends.
Music pours
prodigally
through doors and windows,
the wall
where I am listening, motionless
to catch
a sounding spirit
as its source.

I think the musicians
are happy.
I would like to
applaud,
dare not obtrude
my sound, respect
the silence they make.

cockroach: a tribute

having become accustomed to customs of
cockroaches
their patterns of retreat,
how they learn early
to free fall from walls when hands
approach
how they breed
in neat brown casings found
when empty
their swiftness and persistence, impervious
to sprays, even professional
extermination
dropped from the air
how patiently they wait in plumbing till the water
                                                    stops
Poison the drain:
                        yet
                when I'm sleeping
                they creep up
                to sanctuary
                in wallpaper
                that cracked plaster
                I avoid looking
                    at

schoolday

under my bed
by the wall
I hide from my mother
she is holding
my sister's shoes
mine are at drago's
not ready
kids say
my clothes are
too small or too big
what somebody gave
I hate school
will not wear
the shoes of my sister

moving in

moving in
I see
white faces only
boy staring over
his bike
girl says, hello
it's scary
only white faces
hope
I make friends
we're integrating
the building

Mugging

Ma
I was mugged
going to school.
Kid said
gimme money.
I gave him
a dime
my bus pass.
Next time I'll

walk faster.

doorman

I   the doorman   stand by
air from outside   attend footsteps
make the door   smile open
tell weather   name part of the day
tenants go   both ways
I face
directions   dogs
the carpet   butt-stomped
salute   the super
one hundred fifty apartments
fresh kids   diapermen   mailmen
mind parcels   babies
take messages
wheel the wheelchairs
hold back drunks
don't belong here
and want to

varicosed   with a trussed hernia
in receipt of condolences upon the
death of my uncle
unjustly ticketed for two minutes overtime parking
needy of caps on my lower front teeth
and other teeth
mindful of new shoes that squeeze my
bunions   and the wallet with my
driver's license ten dollars family pictures
picked from my pocket on the IRT subway express
going downtown last Tuesday
I give   a good morning   each morning
people like it   they
don't have to listen   look   even
                                    at the door

morning

I'll put the coffee up then set my hair
that all may be arranged
upon the stairs of silence
ordering its ages and the strands
of fingers ranging on the row-
dividing keys the hands
are peeling skin will wrinkle back
like deckled pages in a book
closed to the opening eye

Conversation

Our windows speak.
You read by a lamp
as I read.

S. R. O.

I am this person S. R. O.
occupant
single
widow in a
narrow room
linoleum carpet
cracked
under my chair
shade drawn
half-open
half-closed
sill watching
gray pigeons
come down to crumbs

into the mirror I said, darling
not meaning my face
crackled

          Grown children
flown like my husband
long dead. Not his face
meant
or others
pensioned here
with   mice
and leaks in the ceiling. At least
no rats. Thankful
for that. No mouse
in the trap. Get
another.
Pigeons, though
are nice.

Cleaning Lady

She cleans my windows
from inside. I know
she is thorough,
honest, appears every Thursday
before nine. I ask
how she's been and
she tells me. I inquire of
her husband,
mention the news
while she waits for opinions,
smiling.

Today I said, really,
bread should be free.
She waited politely
then got her mops, pail,
detergents, brass polish,
lemon oil, cloths, and the
vacuum cleaner with attachments.

She sings as she scrubs
because, I believe, she likes me.
I pay well, but wish just one time
she would see me,
notice
I'm human.

lamentation after jeremiah to exorcise high rental / high rise building scheduled for construction with public funds

solitary city
you weep in the night
over treacherous friends
become enemies
your people sigh
they seek bread

I have lived in
your affliction
it has soured my flesh
battered my bones
it has hedged me about and made my chain heavy
it lies in wait as insatiable lions
in public places

here on this street where
steel grows in a hard ground
fitted with floors of implacable profit
cool as coins
in high pride standing upon
unimportant bodies

rich building
woe unto you if you rise here
this critical space will cave you
into the cave of its cries

on the roof

sky has endings
it will fit
pores
and nerves
making
a nose
my nose
this retina
retain
infinite
imprints
leafwind
cumuli

the eye moves
river
is ocean
one boat
upon it

john wayne's in bed with you, sylvia

john wayne's in bed with you, sylvia
I know   the way you lie back like
I'm a movie screen   wait for
the clinch   some guy to sing
o sole mio on the soundtrack

work my ass off
watch tv
don't bother jesus christ
keep regular
never on relief or
missed a paycheck
out of debt   the car
paid for
your fur coat
contact lenses
and I get
john wayne in bed with you
yet

I came awake

I came awake in the middle of my life
    wife gone to cancer
        son inducted   sent to die
        and did
                not meaning to

a nightmare   a nightmare
    mottled red clotted infected
        bedsores   blood urine
  hemorrhoids beef-raw
      sleep moans   morning
         a stained nightgown
glucose   albumin   plasmate
    sixteen pills daily
        take x-rays   try this now
    prick needles in stick arms
        leg prongs of tumor-big belly
one hundred ten pounds   then
    ninety   then
        eighty
           who ate her up?

take the fate of your time like a man
    without lie or favor
        I did   the war before you
        (that's what I told you
        (she thought I was crazy

a nightmare   a nightmare
    I'll buy
        x-rated movie dreams
women • undamaged • heroes
    stereophonic sound dreams
        chocolate-covered mound dreams
          and dreams of
               milky
                way

overkill

the gun you place
on the table beside me
breathes its late power
into a kiss   I think of

that thief in the snow
snow bleeding around him

defend yourself with death
how much   insures ?

passion without conscience
holds and probes   you promise
never to hurt me

Order

Parents love the children who
    obey them
    children who sit still and
    clasp their hands
    that clasp their lives around them
    like a moat
    those only who have previously entered
    are inside

Children love their parents
    regulated
    placed in strict
    predictabilities
    even undone in
    orderly arrangements
    or else imposed
    on crocodiles who keep the water
    clean

first snow

how many snows have gone down to the yard from my window
white days in darkness
the yard has its own dusk   constantly fallen
one tree set on a second floor terrace

I am looking for
the sled with back rest

you run ahead
pulling me faster
we gleam past hedges   your small feet in new snow
like a surface of clouds
hard to pull through

yet we go up
this chariot of myths
in cold air   endlessly lifting

**lovers
joan of arc statue, 93rd street**

hand of the lover
blooms its black rose
on white shoulder
hand of the other
sheathed
like five black petals
around a pale center

lovers
in the grass
moving among dandelions
and broken winebottles
make a bouquet
of two colors

gather boatcries
take light
chimneysmoke
fumes of fresh dogdung
into their bodies

they are vision
joan of arc on her
stone horse
charging the river
they are wings
two gulls that call
and continue

wishing   (song)

if I could
look upon this street and see
your car parked with the other cars
not marked
by any special sign
but waiting as if
today there might be
time

pretense would grow
a metal plant
a certain auto that shines
in my mind

sometimes, baby I think

sometimes, baby I think
I won't make it
that all the hopeless you and me of it
will succeed
break us apart almost casually
a beansnap

then
that will be that
an end
undignified by anger
backed into
oblique
no less beaten
for it
not happier
it's over
location of pain
to be bypassed
a local stop
still visible by express train going
past

black sugar

man   you say
buy you dog
big as that
a blue bird
a white cat
real diamond
longislandweekend
then
whambam
thanks, friend
buzz off to
westend and
mrs pink plastic
bodyallnylonelastic

hell is
I like you
make me feel
light
get hit with
chickenshit stories
her bellyache
assache
give me gas

I got
heartache
no pills
light bills
man   you say
I suffer
and like to

Mrs. Pink Plastic

Mink keeps me warm.
I have a drink at lunch
with friends
can buy a dress
but won't
I'm fat look bad
in clothes.

Kids grown
gone
my life's gone out
of here.
I'm left with you
might as well be
in the wall
fall break my neck
the plot is ready
even the stone's up
where Momma lies.

I've been
ringed with napkins
unfolded with linens
presented upon china
in crystal
candlesticks used.
                    The gold bird
over the mirror
is watching. A clock ticks
into cachepots, the bookcase with
blue English platters.
Everyone sits.
I am surrounded
surrendered to
occasions.

cold poem 1.

when it's cold
bums go indoors
my kids can play
street is decent
trees up
after years' agitation
for trees
bare now, but improving
the block

cold poem 2.

cold, sister, is
hard on you
standing there
you watch
keep warm at
one a.m.
pacing a doorway
wool scarf on head
wait for some guy with
ten bucks

cold poem 3.   hotel

in Puerto Rico
sun shines kindly
for a coat
we have cousins
like flowers around us
here strangers
and cold
I'm thirty
stock boy in
supermarket
three kids
wife washing diapers
in the sink
always the smell
clothes drying
from steampipe to window
line full except Sunday
my wife so clean
baby cries, her brothers
run and fight

in spring
we can stay
outside

Cop and Robber   (song)

Officer:

      gadgeted with manacles, et cetera
      beneath that costume
      layered cloths like crimes hide
      usual fallibilities.

Know the parts?
      Guard the robber
      prompt a smiling
      mask in his pocket
      you won't let him reach for.
      He wears a glass coat.

You missed the cue
in his navel.

In the Park

I am in the park and
you are in the park
beset by
fences twisted
sharpened at the top.
Swing high
I'll catch you. Crawl
up the slide I'm
with you my hands
at your back.
I am the station
of handkerchiefs.

A boy in the sandbox
hits you
as I sit
with the news.
I see your fist
the future.

Hit back.
Tomorrow is
what it was.

after dinner

when that taxi pulled off
when it lurched from your hand toward the
     white man ten feet away
when it left you standing foot off the curb in a puddle with
     the rain down hard
my just-eaten chow mein dinner lumped under my heart
and I stood under the restaurant awning   hoping :
     male chauvinist
or that the rain and the night were too thick for him to have
     noticed you   on the illuminated street
and I wanted to run to the corner armed
     with my umbrella
     to challenge him
     as he waited   obeying the traffic light

and I waited

Home Movies on Broadway

Here, sound is in the mind. Pictures give me
you, yesterday, a Williamsburg Restoration that
does not change, the change that is not
yet, you, yesterday.

How beautiful. Not only the past
in its nurturing colors, but
today, tomorrow, how
beautiful we are.

Soldiers drill on the lawn.
A cannon utters a white puff.
The people smile and applaud.
Children run.

Outside the screen
night takes
a man's cries
into firecrackers
the insufficient light
of explosions.

Day droops
to empty hands
that clap salvation
at the corner
where something
is waiting
to appear.

imperfections

within series of
inevitable
developments
the world continually
burns, drowns
in fragments
nothing perfect
being part
bright, pale
whole shadows
bodies riven
dry blood and
stagnant water
by tides of
cold clear oceans

everyone dying
puts on child's eyes
like a coat
wonder protects
with innocence
going of daughters
tall sons
blind old men
kind wives
tends the connection
of living
with the dead
and every object
sensed or desired
sperm
ova
endpapers
and promise

**for dana and gregory, explaining somewhat
why we stayed**

they said they were running to
air
air clearly printed with stars
green nerves
flashing keen
within flowers and flesh
headed upward
sunward
the snow glowing high
impeccably white

we watched them go

under dust
of energy or despair
our streets lie
dung-dappled
mixed cries from
faces jumbled in
embrace, brawls
forms and hues
whose mingling is
the rolling flow of space

places of the mind
are mottled
dipped with a delicate eye
into thoughts
of small gradations
weighted by
a thousand separate
sound waves
and
sensual motion
refining
defining
extending

antinomy

I am learning myself
as passage
doorway without doors
how to crawl through myself
emerging with a permanent squint

yet steady
the harsh distance throughout

fulcrum

there is a resolution turning all my thought
to act
as a kernel of wheat intending what is fed
and to the world of tables and temptations
I oppose this noise

it is camping outside stillness
it is a roaring touch that will not leave you
as it revolves its force and facets
to your cold eye

there is a revolution turning all my thought
to armies
to the worn and passive hand at last accepting
within its wrinkled pulse the metal chamber
poised upon
its turn

on heroes, hero-worship
footnote to Carlyle

some poets
go abroad
to borrow
make myths
navigate genitalia
graves of old gods

heroes here
are myths
their summoning acts
shout life from the lips of
loud tombs

my place to praise
the moral station
this street my muse
raising rag banners
to the general will

fierce land   of
desperate saints

for kay leslie

kay leslie, yours the length:
a hundred marches here
and washington
for peace
a black stream
voters bravely
registering
in mississippi

tears of others touch
your brown eyes
vulnerable
having lost much
yet you fill
thin frames of spirits
like sparrows
around whom you rise
a fountain

for max and isabel manes*

max and isabel
no peace
but poor people
exist
on and on
an incandescent
poverty
flicked on
by systems

dim light .
to work by

but
pattern
is born
in the eye
of a needle
hopethreaded
lifting to stitch
the west side
                of the world

* founders: west side committee on vietnam
                friends of the welfare rights organization
                seniors for adequate social security (SASS)

for Max and Isabel Manes, poem revised

Listen, Max
I've written you and Isabel another poem.
The first was tersely poetic, whereas
you are lively and generously conversational
and constantly renewing, expanding your lives.

This edition, therefore,
reviews you both
as you teach us to grow
SASSy power.
The lines remain about
unemployed, underpaid people
their incandescent poverty
flicked on and on by political systems,
how by that dim light you labor
knowing pattern is born
in the eye
of a needle
hopethreaded
lifting to stitch
the west side
        of the world

Dissident Poet

In my kitchen, O dissident poet
you declaim your classification
like a proud Star of David
imposed on your
gesturing hand
its middle finger
blasted by gunfire
in a past war.

for jennette washington*

jennette
you're mad as hell
at almost everyone
stay mad
keep that hard rage
dry as a stone
in your fist
give none of it
away

defend yourself
the street's not safe
you'll be raped
with promises
vote stolen
no redress
they'll say it's just
the local
high crime rate

so
on guard, jennette
keep that hard rage
dry
give none of it
away

*formerly eastern regional director, national welfare rights
organization

margaret cook::

posters   leaflets   yourself going out to the day at the corner
ideas like a long poem spinning into the telephone
walking around as if truth had a spine that could keep you
from tiring

so little time, now
for repose

sleep closes imperfectly
there is always a dream
attending

incident at st. gregory's, april 21, 1970

father browne father browne
they hunt the priests here
the altar is bristling with
bows and arrows
carbines
and catapults
spears
and slingshots
grenades
and napalm
and bombs
and tear gas
and nerve gas
and plagues
the ancient rocks of hate in their hands
their hearts are rocks under their ribs
holy water runs blood in the fountain
stones of the church bleed
babies like rainbows bleed
and the guillotined minds of men are dumped
into wastebaskets

father browne father browne
they'll break the church door down
        they will have to break it down
        to take berrigan

father browne father browne
the reichstag is burning
        we'll fight any fire
        and build again

father browne father browne
they're invading the world
    they've been here before
    and we've fought them
    they will die
    we will die
    but when struggle
    structures our souls
    then
    we are free

panther

black as the sun I live under
in the heat of my life
black as the earth that has burned
and the stars that are burning
black as ice on the world
apocalyptic
my visions
arm me
with steel roses

in the jungle
I wear a white suit
in offices I crawl
through glass doors

they say
that man has black fur

I will claw
suckle
strike monuments
and men
with paradoxes
learned
by the terrors and furies
of my wounds
I must be animal
toward man
a man
among animals

I number my days
like pages
and wake to dim mornings
my story revised in newspapers
white lies for others

I drink coffee from chipped cups
my coat is open to winter
I have winds to ride
and a storm coming

now is my time to receive
every hunter who seeks me

I am here   in the clearing

CORRECTION, PLEASE

charged with the news of this world
come at me in screams
    IT HAS HAPPENED
       AGAIN
          AGAINST THEM (ragbare to rages
                     (the torn thighs
                        (and

W E   B U R N

(Recognizing in the paper the charred holes of my eyes
I telephone the *Times*
   tell them
     W E   A R E   B U R N I N G
I tell *The New York Times* that we are burning that
  the pictures somehow mixed up are not Oriental
or the grass hut captioned Vietnamese
C O R R E C T I O N , P L E A S E   none of your fine print, either

CORRECTION

60 POINT CENTURY BOLD ITALIC

none of your business I mean none of your
8½ point imperial roman regular print
    regular type face

THIS IS IRREGULAR   THE WHOLE THING STINKS   BELIEVE ME
HIGHLY IRREGULAR to have reported the semblance of news
the type of face it has

    not what it is

IT IS AN OUTRAGE

Happening again, against them, ostensibly, but facts
ARE NOT FIT TO PRINT facts get on the hands the white gloves
though one hears of BABIES DELIVERED ON NEWSPRINT (another conception of germs

YOU MUST PRINT THE TRUTH, MR. TIMES, I GIVE TO YOU STRAIGHT
WITH FREE TRIAL OFFER EXAMINE THE HOLES OF MY SKULL YOU ARE WRITING ABOUT
R E C O G N I Z E M E !
THE AMERICAN FLAG WITH TWO HOLES IN IT
A BABY WITH TWO HOLES IN IT
A MOUNTAIN WITH TWO HOLES IN IT
T H E C R O S S T O W N B U S

LISTEN TO ME, NEW YORK TIMES, YOU'VE GOT IT ALL WRONG
Please, prudently print corrections—any way you like—
today, tomorrow, soon, soon

is ethical

up here

up here
the action is real
people shot out of cannons
are blown up
they walk with lions
who eat them
dance a tightrope
that breaks
and the clowns cry
and the popcorn tastes bitter

up here
switchbladed laughter
pricks at skin
better run
it will slice you
down to mouths
studding the ground like pores

long hunger
bred us cannibal
better run fast
wrath is here
wrath is
anything near

The Blue Man

At last he rose and twitch'd his mantle blew;
To morrow to fresh woods, and pastures new.
from *Lycidas,* by John Milton

Summoning the snow
Aeolus of blue sheet winding
a spiral of air about
your purple hat with its star
that testifies
to the greatness of Allah
and blesses me as I pass

Blue Man —
pilgrim of broom handle staff
mu'ezzin come out of mosque tower
call us into faith
its "mantle blew"
that touches your shoulders, also
with love and myth
and a distant, sacred art

CHILDREN OF THE HOUSE AFIRE /
More Notes on 94th Street

D. H. Melhem: A Reassessment

D. H. Melhem's *Children of the House Afire / More Notes on 94th Street* brings us all a widening of that pellucid lens which she displayed in *Notes on 94th Street;* a welcome extension of that book's falcon-eyed, darting candor of vision. These further notes gain, I think, in major part from the richly meditative fluency of Melhem's intervening book, *Rest in Love,* in which she considered, and laid forth to us, her own history's terrain. This act of expansion, I believe, enabled or at least facilitated the ampler observation of the present book; which releases its figures into a more carefully surveyed and articulated terrain, and admits more direct entry of the poet, self-delivered from the omniscient detachment of the earlier book so that her very sensibility, seen in devices like the occasional literary allusions, becomes a more positive factor of identification. The archetypal and prototypal figures—the Black Panther, the Pink Plastic Lady—of the earlier *Notes,* here give place to figures in a landscape: the universal emblems to one's fellow citizens, delineated by the skein of their actions. Figures like the street musicians, in one of the current poems, whose art, with its manifold fluent components, liberates them from the enclosure of illustration. Finally, the increased spaciousness and more leisurely rhythms allow for the surfacing of a vital motif which was largely implicit, or muted, in the earlier book: the heroic self-propelling energy of nature, the restoring signal to our lives, however frail its form, and however brutal, blind and destitute the ground through which it must thrust. *Children of the House Afire* is an ardent yet faultlessly disciplined poetic journal, which is given indispensable focus and dimension by the presence of the poet herself.

Donald Phelps

with love to

Dana   Gregory   Roslynn   Louis

John   Allen   Yang Ja   Douglas

Margaret

Claudia   Jim   Ree   Peggy   Arthur

Olga   Kay   Isabel   Max

also Homer

and the City of New York

embattled, gallant, enduring

MICROCOSM

Window Notes

to the sun

o sun
isn't it difficult
to get down to this street
through the dust of all wars
the unfinishing wailing

there is no way directly between us
except by affiliation
survivors among stumps, earthclot
shellholes locking their losses

window woman

1.

having nothing but garbage
to give to this street
you spit out the window
you throw a paper bag into a pile of cartons

small and old
you tuck the cold light coming at you as a child,
                                          a complaint
into your white kerchief
staining the glass

you never come down

here, more and more, confined to dimensions
framed in a similar way against the view
will I, too, one day remain ascended
into the fierce discrepancies of the heart

2.

They threw your furniture out the window.
Nobody wanted it. Your son the restaurant-owner
didn't want it. Your bed broke
from the second floor
and the sofa collapsed in an aura of dust.
They tied up your brooms and mop
and put them by the fence on a pile of things.
I see your white kerchief
in the glint of a dingy light
against the glass.

Strangers

We look through our blinds.
    I look out and
    you look.

Nothing to see in this courtyard:
    barred windows, cats,
    backs of air conditioners.
    Nothing to see but
the other.

I won't know you tomorrow
    on the street. Embarrassing
    to meet, having shared
the sly moment:
    invisible hands
    lifting a slat.

It's like friendship
    your being there.

We make
no demands.

two versions of a plane tree

1.

plane tree
your sensuous branches
dip over the terrace fence
their partial escaping
while above, to the top, erect
facing roofs
you maintain a stance:
positioned, predictable
staunch, and confined

2.

this breeze is tragical, a flaw in the season
a minimal scratch though palpable
upon those leaf-plucked branches that still seem
full of summer   appearances that are
what they are and were   and more
being in motion always
to compose themselves   in my perishing eye
they scatter   fluttering
like shades in Dante and in Virgil
souls   in the visible leaves

Screamer:

you screamed your lonely rage
up this block
then dyed your hair blonde
and were quiet
I saw you today with a friend
the first one ever with you on the street
and her hair was dyed blonde, too
I am so happy for you!

winter woman

winter woman in july
you wear a coat, scarf, gloves, boots
protection

subway

    night in the station
       small lights in the wall
          day breaks
          into places
             to move toward

express

    the impact: bone —
    blood in the trough of the track
    a head collapsing on steel
    staining our wheels
    the implacable train of us . . .

trackman
for robert burns

that gray mouse avoids you .
through the light of your cap
does your head see a glare impending its colors
                                      that send you to a wall
                             you become small
                    a smudge on tile
ignored by harsh cars
the mouse cornered beneath
and you thinking the train might
sway

we move through dim and sudden tunnels
with platforms here and there
           splattered islands
                          depressed tracks

ON STRIKE
Local 32B, April 1976

When I saw you, doorman
detaining the United States mail truck
I thought revolution
begins like this:
two people
one saying, No!

workman

in the shade of a fire escape
on a 90° street
you stand eating a cheese sandwich

the young tree nearby indicates
another place you might be
and it might, if not for having been
set there as, in some measure
you are

on the street

these men are all on crutches — invisible
see how they clutch
at buildings   the rough stone
that steadies them   the touch
necessary   not love
just being there

Toward a redistribution of wealth

The red eyes of police cars flash and turn
like buoys in a dreadful harbor.

At night: thief's blood on the lobby door —
a sacrificial scrawl on glass
visible from both sides.

The problem for the doorman is
to keep death out.

ginkgo

Coming up from the street to me: ginkgo!
Five years — you're at my window now and upward
How I love your wild arms — every way flapping — beckoning!

from my window

red hair singing behind her head   she runs with her dog
slim in their shanks and the length of anticipation
longshadowed before the sun

gray hairs over my eyes
streak my perception
of a few certain things

       you,

        running as if in slow motion
        blue jacket ballooning in the wind
        a man beautiful for a man
        who waits for you on a traffic island
        as you pace homeward, having remembered
        something to do or take
        some bridge, perhaps, to him

to the symphony theater

people fall
they lie down in a desperate street
pavement cracks drily
ginkgo trees twist their branches

along sharp bodies we zigzag to the theater
that stands among men who totter
against each other

when the movie lets out
we pass them quickly
hold fast to images
packaged inside us

electrician
for claudia

Adam
walking with his toolbox   he stoops a little, now
when I first met him he was thirty and thin
could fix things   worked in the hardware store
not wanting his own business   it was convenient
to be employed by old people who liked him

today a green man commands him   Adam
his garden of wires, nuts, screwdrivers
and hammers   to ply his instructions

once
he put up my chandelier   leaned deeply
into the crystal   the light at his hands
his reflecting eyes: blue-white

I see him trudging
down a long and final street
to lustrous occasion
sparkling seed

riverside

by the fence
on a bench
I look down

the river
is a presence
the ball game
is played
bordered by strollers
warm dogs
children in heightening swings

above me pigeons perch
in families /
on the ground
they preen

park mother

a park mother may suspect
that the other child in the sandbox
will continue to throw
indiscriminate grains

The Harlequin Lady

Two boys tease the Harlequin Lady. She who does not speak is standing in the middle of Broadway, screaming at them. As the cars and trailers of commerce screech before her, she will not be moved. She is telling the offense, confronting it with two weary shopping bags filled with fabrics and ribbons, shreds of a lifetime, stuffed into paper.

The Harlequin Lady is bravely adorned with red, green, and white; her stockings are striped horizontal. She wears a red hat and a green hat and brass coins and beads. Sometimes she jingles. She lives on 94th Street and walks up from the river. I am glad she berates the boys who have frightened her.

I and my unknown neighbors, those who hang out at the corner, speak briefly of the woman, and the boys I, too, have scolded; of how the world is unfit for innocuous people; and how the harsh games of children are those of their elders and have set an old black woman in the middle of Broadway to defy heavy traffic.

in the street

3:00 a.m.

        backed against the car
        hands up

           the Korean mute accuses you
in his guttural cry
and the aproned clerk shakes his fist
while the policeman snaps your hands
into handcuffs
a curse leaps free
from your clenched soul

        as you enter
        the police car

on 137th street

to make this street bloom geraniums
clay pots parallel trash cans downhill
over garbage
dogs ascending to the corner
that sits
watchful in weather
water and trees
at the end of it
boats going away
smoke leftover

you
combing your hair
at a third-floor window
tide of an unborn child
shifting the cloth of your dress
a man downstairs
observes you

the river
restless

Pigeonlady

Pigeonlady
from the park :

bring birds
to this street

your index
they follow to
breadsack you carry

cast crumbs
bring birds
to this street

capitalism

1. the girls

The girls out there are young and scared
stand tall on platform shoes
their pimps at the corner in phone booths
watching

Walking my dog at night I, too, am scared
the crazies must march their torments
that crowd them in small rooms,
the junkies must find pushers
and the drunks disgorge their anger

The girls out there —
set on the block at intervals
stone-eyed
caryatids of their littered turf

I pass them
pimps watching

2. pimps: from the Library glass-enclosed patio

We sit, talking. The girls in the rain
beyond our glass, our caul
walk delicately with umbrellas
as if balancing something of value
on high wires.

Across the street, four pimps stand
under an awning::
they are splendid in silver and sharkskin
and broad-brimmed hats and rings and canes
and high platform shoes to gauge
their merchandise offered from that level
their gaze like strings like wires pulled taut
for the girls to walk on.

Politics:
a declamation with demurrers

MY PARTY * I INVITE

to lion games, the long circular course
where chariots race, horse against horse.
So I will turn you all to face ahead,
infuse with future: terminals and the dead.

I FURTHERMORE   PROPOSE
to talcum history between the toes.

. . .

Go to. . .
You are not, forsooth, the truth.
Gadzooks and zounds! Take that, you villain
in your soundtrack, schmuck. Your luck is good
we don't prick your tires, your
heart, that olive
stuffed with your desires.

. . .

Got a nice crowd on this corner. Half
waiting for a fix. The rest
curious, confuse
your noise with action.
Tell us, man, just why
this lady here's a whore, and how
my room gets heat this winter, where
the rats will go, and when
you'll stop your lies and be
a bum out of a job, like me.

Children of the House Afire:

To the seven children and three adults who died
in the fire at 311 West 94th Street, February 4, 1976,
and to the survivors

There you stand: empty building
with broken eyes
clay pots on your sills
plaster saints in a window
and a drapery fluttering burnt flowers
the residue of music, pots and pans
and families clustering to eat and sleep
behind the fire escape /
today smoke lingers here unseen
in the blood

Children —
flames were the red mountain of your cries
the cries of poor children, heard too late,
huddled in a room for help to come

Children —
you who wore a confirmation dress last May
gone to the white smoke clouds
after firemen's hoses
gone to the black smoke raging your pain
gone down fire escapes crowded with
weeping and falling and waiting

Help reaches through the hands of neighbors
it covers cold flesh with a blanket
it finds shoes and shelter
for strangers thrown
to wet snow

Children —
you who have given to grief its undeserved portion
let your charred and monstrous gift yet give to us
a new way of seeing this street
may we hear its crowded sorrows
may the sound pour compassionate streams
upon all this burning city
and with a light of many colors
fill the gutted structures
where we live

Love Notes

love notes

outside: rain —
awakening with you:
good weather!

how carefully you strike words for me
that go to blue flame!

the truth of us   eye to eye
your face above me

I wish I had many years with you
instead of this
narrow
rushing

so big, this affection
like a big, comfortable person
with a kind face
your face

bed of love: I kiss
the very bed of love

what I want to get at in you
is that private soul of no entry
to meet my own —
that you I have glimpsed
like a terrain of stars
in their scintillant magnitudes . .

.

trio:
I and solitude and you

what to do:
I can't help being
older than you

brown crystal flesh
where the edge of every hue
and pulse and cry
is tested

your face
delicate and gentle upon me
draws outward my own will
the curve of your spine is freckled under my fingers
I feel many colors there   beneath your ribs

o body —
like a rutabaga or radish or rose or refuse —
must you decay?

the years   how they round the curve   and drop away like
the wooden horse at steeplechase park
years and corners ago
drop down drop off
the years

you said:
take my love with you. I took it
amulet, everywhere
and brought it back
increased

where did you go?

already
losses
grow
classical
an open
temple
peripteral

poems
to someone
not there
but
could be

switchblade   you cut me
why don't you call?

the losses
pounding me pestle me
bit by flesh to dust

Watching the Tall Ships on the Hudson
July 4, 1976

in the photograph
watching the tall ships the tall ships
slowly grandly distantly
as memory fills their sails and they move up river
farther from the heart farther into dim glimmering pastness

you and I at the river
watching the tall ships
we are smiling I love you
(how can this be?
you are counterfeit —
I love my own thoughts about you)
nevertheless
gone gone
sailed away — sunk

You, Me, and Wallace Stevens's "The Snow Man"

Night approaches from the north
wearing your serpentine shoes
you swirl around
my vulnerabilities

my eyes are holes clear through
my head's a rattle
I stand mouth open to the wind
with all the misery in it

a child's cry whirls down the galaxy
into my throat where a woman mourns
and a man who has lost everything
calls out his wager

For a troubled friend

You come to me
from the street and the stars
in your camel's hair coat
your brown eyes with a long and eloquent
sadness from all the streets
their woes and violence, and the aspiration
in blue, outlined in clouds.
You say, there is a cloud about me.
You feel this vagueness almost strangeness
to yourself. I see
a glory round your head, the dazzle
on a mountain, a possibility
of vision which is my heart's
language. Something of you
is frozen at the root
and sleeps like an old man
on church steps.
I would kiss this man awake
to an altar of windowed light
and the high slopes of love.

L., asleep

even when your face goes slack
and a sliver of gold glints from a tooth
and you snore with a deep, trusting depth
the sweet gesture of your body's repose
turned slightly, spills its love

there is no withholding —
for me, for the sheets, for the room
into the prepositions of embrace
breath, an embrace, a dream

the globe of the lamp does not
contain the light
but gives it to you

I touch your beating heart
to have a certain knowledge of it

The Cool Swan

We speak
toward the limit of affection
where you leave me
in the passage that must move
like water glancing
from the neck of a cool swan

A black swan and a white swan
meet and meet
in the lake of circular shores
where each may find
its reeds and shelter

Sometimes I think you are
all the black swans in the world
having been disdained
now utterly disdaining
proffered bread   proffered fish
loaves that can be shared without limit
fish that multiply as they are taken

I plunge my head
open my eyes in the water
to what is cast there
before it falls
to the bottom
and what may swim about my feet

You   a moving light
in the darkness of your feathers
in the deepening of your distance
attend   another shore

ROSE POEMS

the dying call us

have been filled with your dying
felled by the glance of love
before the grave

those unused days dry salt now
fall with you
brim a hole
in the ground

Wedding-Day, January 17, 1970

Mother mother
is that you
in Rose's bed?
You wear her face —
bones hold
her bouquet.
Smile
over her eyes
and the music

O Promise Me.

Dear Aunt, Upon Your Wedding

Lovely Rose, go blithely
into flowers.

Our faces
ring you. The groom
wears new shoes. His moustache
kisses you crisply.
He cradles
your loosening bones.

at st. vincent's

roses
red
your buttocks
red
red tongues of your eyes
in a white box room
cover for pain

stems turn skeletal
in morphine

you pray for reasons
I give you roses

brimming the chalice of that pillow
your amazed head sets it pain
swollen walls
crowd the footboard
and the boiling bed
screams
its dissolving bones

from one closed eye
beneath the hair-line tumor
a tear moves

comatose
do you dream?

be Cho Cho San
upon a stage
this page your notice
to heaven

before bravas
utter your rosary
lustrously sing

rosie
struggling
snoring and rattling carry on
the hard business
dying

coffin shuts
on lies and
the loving
a ventriloquist soprano
gives you jocelyn's berceuse

star at last
in an eastern star production
the green dress you wanted
the song

to the music of rose and henry

I hear you
    the screened music
        needle notes   bars   guitars
muted into morphine   madame butterfly
      pinned to a perpetual singing   into
my winged head   stone heavy with
        hopeful relics   my hair steel-strung
over my eyes that carry your full color
    to the air of my wrung spirit weeping your graces
      I hear you

rose
your cats ate lobster   you were poor   you dyed your hair black
and your husband ate cream cake with false teeth
he wore spats and played golf
and drew sporting goods for abercrombie catalogs
until they used photos
and he played for you

there was never an assurance in your singing
but you aspired
and took courage late
and sang at christmas for sick people
in hospitals
we heard you on the radio and wrote letters to the station
you borrowed money   over wine you cried for your mother
who sat at the table downstairs with your brothers and sisters
eating your homemade cheesecake with uncle henry
who laughed, embarrassed

I hear you

and when I listen to puccini
or the persistence of a distant guitar
knowing the notes without sound that
can never approach me
though I may swoop and soar to the utmost reverberations
I listen, I listen, and I hear you

MACROCOSM

poems:
the oceanic embrace of the world

poems:
in the pale air you shine
you say your perspectives
tell me what I am
you take up the things themselves
you respect
life

New York Times, **August 15, 1976**
"As Lebanon Dies"

my background is lebanese
and peaceful, I said
proud of redundancy

grandmother beirut
grandfather damascus
my father tripoli
on the clear coast, a boy
diving for sea-urchins

now the tides cast
their dead blossoms
to sprawl at the roots of cedars
whose ancient tongues
weep fire in the sun

On the tendency toward solipsism in literature

1.

Where am I in your poems?
How can you be there without
the boundary defining you — the place
we are accomplishing? Are you
a blob, unmanageable endless omnivore,
a science fiction fact, the total topographical
of earth, a mobile constellation, quirky quasar,
voluminous vegetal omniscient—
how about that?
Where are you leading — except
to Parmenides, his circle
spherically flat?

2.

The unimpassioned poem is retrospective of a flight
responsible only to
its own hovering images that link
Ming vases with the tense
of made things, of mental surfaces, and with feelings
shaped to the fixed glaze of a tight, washable glisten.
Feathers can dust the unimpassioned poem
where nothing
importunately clings

but the poem whose rude textures
grapple with the live space
around the self
can grip the air
and hold light, and fly
as the earth flies

for Seurat, his "Sunday Afternoon on the Island of la Grande Jatte"

Enclosed in the dream la Grande Jatte
caught in its utter calm
still profile of the day
filtered by memory
created in place
dreamers sit
or poise upon grass
where, like trees
their verticals, rooted, serenely rise.

**for Greg and Roslynn
at Woods Hole**

This is the house that life may enter.
Here a pet hermit crab, in borrowed gold,
draws its shell over pebbles in a bowl.
A spider webs a lintel
and a squirrel, caught in the pantry,
is released. Blackbirds pry,
and birds in blue and silver.
A gull floats high.

Nothing disturbed:
the small, the moderate in size
or circumstance, the giant pin oak
in its power and plunging roots
and vital springs, the sense that
no moth or flame of perception,
about this house, is negligible.

for margaret, at ninety-three, convalescing

in this pause
the words   the doing
defined with art
work in the world
your clear identity

you open each day
to the light in your room
of crystal energies
that scan newspapers
like signals
you relay
stationed by a green lamp
reading

on the rejection of an attica prisoner
for funeral rites, september 18, 1971

O priest at the highest incense of your justice
accept for burial this reject
attica man
do not turn the signs of your chasuble
against him
or raise the sacramental cup
to a private sanctum

death
is a public matter

For An Old Woman Killed In The Monterey Hotel, October 30, 1975

Defended by metal lock and metal chain
hoping to move tomorrow
down the block
in faith that this city might still
accommodate the small intrusion
of your sheltering,
you lived for years where even the fear
was familiar, and you could recognize
a solace in mortality —
that sinister shadowing to your door
until it lengthened there,
and entered.

Old woman, my hand has touched
the handle of the blade
that finished you

leviathan

> — One great society alone on earth:
> The noble Living and the noble Dead.
>   William Wordsworth, *The Prelude*, Book XI

it is the old trick
machiavelli told, did not invent
but verified as the best method to dispose of
opposition:
                    kill them
                    get every leader
                    jail first   if you must   then
                    like an image that recurs upright
                                        in a shooting gallery
there   for that moment   you aim
(Canst thou draw out leviathan with a hook?)

sometimes it takes long
ten years to get
george jackson
he was difficult, brazen in pain
connected ideas
himself   his jail cell
with the wild malignancy
outside
(Canst thou put a hook into his nose? or bore his jaw through
with a thorn?)

in areopagitica, john milton
said   christian belief
spread without scripture
the inquisition
imprisoned galileo
not what he knew
(Hugest of living Creatures, on the deep
Stretchd like a Promontorie sleeps or swimmes)

last year I read in a paper:
amman battle drags as
guerrillas resist
fighting has increased intensity
camps now under
close-range bombardment
(By art is created that great Leviathan, called a Commonwealth
or State . . . which is but an artificial man.)

It is one conflict always
my great-grandfather's beard
wagged red in battle
I carry his banner

> the whale
> endures
> her tail
> is an ocean
> look look / she sings
> a child streams
> from her eyes
> and water
> upon water
> clings

on bombing one's own troops erroneously

who's bombing who —
whom? them
they were there, well
should have been
elsewhere

to george jackson   (a dirge)

george jackson-o-o-o-oh
george jackson-o-o-o-oh
when did they give you that gun
did they put it in your hand when you lay
dead in the sun

george jackson-o-o-o-oh
when did they give you that gun
did they put it in your mother's womb
to bear with her son

george jackson-o-o-o-oh
when did they give you that gun
did they forcefeed their hate until
you became one :

                    a gun
                         george jackson

song for angela davis
in the women's house of detention

angela davis angela davis
body is caged
but your mind goes out to the street
as a panther passing through stone
staining ground with immovable shadows

truth is
that last light in the eye of pain
will not close with the lid of a coffin
until every grave empties its light
every gutter runs grief to the sewer
until grief is flowing free
around every island
and the world drowns in unused dreams
and the world drowns in unused dreams

for Delacroix, his "Liberty Leading the People"

A king was taking strong measures:
he attempted to swallow the press
he gnawed the vote down to the bone
of wealthy landholders
and made himself law —
but the press stuck in his gullet
till he gagged
republicans whacked him between the shoulders
and he coughed —
Charles the Tenth who ran
from the image of Liberty
which moves in the Delacroix painting.

Louis Philippe was gracious for a time.
He praised peace and order,
but soon he was taking strong measures.
He feared the painting
and had it put into storage
like Louis Napoleon after him.

But Liberty fled her museum
invaded the Tuileries
took over the Assembly
in 1848.

Marx and Engels had issued their *Manifesto,*
our conestoga wagons charged westward
for gold —
it was a battered Liberty we dragged to California
harnessed with horse teams pulling us over
the Indians
away from half-enslaved lands.

"Liberty Leading the People,"
her banner clarities of red, blue, and white
wash over the white flag of the Bourbons.
In the foreground, several are fallen.
At the base of the barricade
the Swiss, the cuirassier
republican and royalist
clutch their common death.

Liberty, grasping her musket, her banner,
marches across the barricade
glancing backward
signalling advance
exuberant
in the child at her side,
in the force of form
infusing her followers
whose blood will stream
from her eyes!

Delacroix:
your painting says to us,
History, history that is true —
not only the splattered bombast
of kings and generals
the bloodless decisions
that bloody the nations
but the whole canvas of conflict
where sorrows lie
in confused colors of earth and death,
and ordinary men and women
are raised and moved
to restore themselves.

To the son of julius and ethel rosenberg
at the village gate

Son of julius and ethel rosenberg
I saw you at the village gate on a stage last night
your hair streaming like long tears of the past
1953 when you were a child
and your parents were strapped into burning chairs
for our benefit, and died with their protests of innocence
searing a road for you in the land

Now, as you raise money
to reopen the case and the cause of your mother and father
they whose large pictures are drawn on the flag of this country
against which your living figure is foregrounded
and they, in turn, move a little before you in an air
which can never be tasted
no matter how keenly you stretch all your senses
and your child's heart cries out to them
in its faithful arms from the roots of your manhood
I think of your pain, and how children
must bear the spores and seeds of their parents' vitality
in themselves and their children and populate the earth
with inherited knowledge

How large are the faces of julius and ethel rosenberg
on that fragile cotton flag
they are bigger than faint stars or the stripes like whips
bigger than the stage, they soar over bitter judgments
over the earth like red and blue figures
in a painting by chagall
as they open the gate to a village
of thatched hopes and bread and vines of hands
offering compassionate fruit

attention

returning the earthworm to the grassy border
I tapped it lightly with my pavement shoe
yet crushed   some part of it

things are more delicate (or strong)
within the edges   of our expectations

REQUIESCANT 9/11

September 11, 2001, World Trade Center, Aftermath

1.

Under a hard blue sky
a white shroud rises.

Uptown
air turns acrid.
I close my windows.

Cloud messages
from the plume of hell,
I breathe you, taste the mist —
concrete dust, chairs, shoes,
files, photos, handbags, rings, a doll,
upholstery, breakfast trays,
body parts and parting words
and screams.

Blood of workers, passengers, police —
O firemen running up stairs
past people streaming
from a tower poised to crash —

I breathe you flowing
into the ceaseless sacrifice
of innocents.

My TV exhales frantic images:

Have you seen her? Have you seen him?
Everybody loved her. He was my friend.
Anybody seen them?

Anger rolls over grief and prayers.
"Vengeance!" echoes from toxic caves.

Like spores of a giant fungus,
rage races through the air.
"Vengeance!" the people cry.
All die again.

2.

Union Square Park, Two Weeks Later:
A Pilgrimage

Sunday,
a day as sunny as that other.
Slowly, beneath the trees,
along wire fences garlanding the grass
with flowers, candles, prayers,
love messages on colored papers, photographs,
I walk with vigilant mourners winding past.

Level with branches, George Washington,
astride a horse, carries a fireman's flag
and a peace flag tipped red with a Valentine heart:
"One people."
Invocations anoint his pedestal:
"Love One Another, Give Peace a Chance."

Seated before him on the ground,
Buddhists in unison strike their prayer drums.
Nearby, a couple collect for the Firemen's Fund.
Across the park, pipers and drummers
march past Abraham Lincoln,
proclaim "The Battle Hymn of the Republic."

Later, in a drugstore stocked with filter masks
I buy a box. Each one disclaims protection
from toxic dust and poison gas.

Drawn to my City's visible wound
I go downtown.
The subway's nearly empty. I climb
into streets without traffic, buildings powdered white.
Tourists and residents aim their cameras.

On Fulton Street
I join the pilgrimage downhill.

Mask ready, I taste the faintest breath
of acrid smoke, invisible incense
of cries and clamor
still peopling the air.
A woman pulls a suitcase,
a man pulls his.
Which one returns to a ghost apartment,
which one flees?

I reach the crowd and Broadway barricades.
Girders, twisted and wrenched into a pile,
lie helpless beside a jagged crater.
Distant survivor buildings at the rim
face the great square of chaos
a sixteen-acre graveyard. Earth
must have birthed canyons like this,
quaking tectonic rage.

A yellow crane poises high
in homage to the standing shell —
that spire, that Coliseum,
Tower of Pisa leaning grief
against a phantom Twin.

Ground Zero, ground of martyrs, crushed and burned,
their screaming blood bones ashes pulverized
into cement clouds wind carries
through the city to the world.
The crowd, in hushed and rumbling awe,

slows down to get a better view.
"Keep moving!" a bullhorn shouts.

Into the roiling space
an old sign on a building calls:
A GOOD TIME TO INVEST!

A policeman who had been there from the first
explains to a visitor why people jumped from windows,
those whom a child had witnessed
as birds afire. I wonder if
they'd wildly hoped for flight.

We speak of gratitude.
"I feel the love," he says.

The air falls heavier.
I press a mask against my nose.
My eyes smart a little.
I pass the glass façade of an empty store.
On pedestals, new shoes
display their dust.
A lone pub signals with a scrawl,
"We're Open!"

My skin begins to hurt.
I need to find a subway,
take home
my heartload.

The train shuns regular stops.
At 96th Street
I find a trash can,
throw the mask away.

Epilogue, *Earth Speaks*

You blast omnivorous graves
where millions in memory lie,
you foul my pleasant air,
you level my mountains of ore.

With greed your guiding law,
and vengeance as your creed,
your justice is suspect,
your mercy is select.
All life deserves respect.

Confront the suffering
you mutually inflict.
Share your crusts of bread—
loaves will multiply.
Staunch my terrible wounds
and heal your own thereby.

Let barren hearts accept
seeds from compassionate rain.

Love is the sternest prayer.
All life deserves respect.

Mindful Breathing

"In the Buddhist tradition, we have the practice of mindful breathing, of mindful walking, to generate the energy of mindfulness. It is exactly with that energy of mindfulness that we can recognize, embrace, and transform our anger. . . ."
—Thich Nhat Hanh, Riverside Church, September 25, 2001

I sit by the window,
concentrate on breathing
and become, breath by breath,
a part of breath, drawn
first from this side of the street
bent to shadows dropped
from a scrawny moon.
Now the whole street is breath
flowing uptown
ebbing downtown
to swirl and swirl around
Ground Zero and blur into smoke
from those buried walls and those bodies,
smoke lifting from deep levels
of caves where survivors are hunted
and none can be found,

yet each one remains,
transformed into breath,
a tower, a vortex,
a silent tornado
or a slow wisp of smoke
curling around light bulbs
and the dark pit
of memory
the pit of my stomach that
rejects this air.
It feels natural and wrong to use it
to keep my body intact, unless
each breath be taken in prayer.

I pray for the smoke of Ground Zero
and the smoke over Afghanistan
and every cinder of human history,
I pray that my own breath embrace
the blame and the connections
to wounded and wounding animals
who die, fall, and rise
into the furnace of living.

Lines Composed a Few Miles above St. Paul's Chapel, and beside the Viewing Platform, Ground Zero, July 4, 2002

> *. . . For I have learned*
> *To look on nature, not as in the hour*
> *Of thoughtless youth; but hearing oftentimes*
> *The still sad music of humanity,*
> *Nor harsh nor grating, though of ample power*
> *To chasten and subdue.*
> — William Wordsworth, from "Lines composed a few miles above Tintern Abbey, on revisiting the banks of the Wye during a tour, July 13, 1798"

Towers explode their lives into the churchyard.
Dust stops the clocks and stills the bells,
turns every surface gray, whips through the graves
and crashes a London plane tree against headstones.

Dust storms the church. Emergency workers
wipe ash and blood from their faces, track heavy prints
inside and scuff the pews with boots and belts
where they rest, leave marks "of their ministry,"
as the vicar said, "their sacramental marks."
                              Emergency!
The Dust weeps, trembling the Great Seal
of the United States presiding from
a wall. Chaos bit by bit subsides
into supplies and food dispensed beneath
the organ gallery—400 meals
each day for workers desperate to find
comrades alive, then grateful to discover
any dead.
                    In the graveyard
spirits kindled in pity rise to accept
the sudden company and wail with them
and weep the world anew. "Has life learned nothing
in two hundred years?" the buried ask,
invite, "Rest here. There's room."

                        "We are innocent!"
the Dust cries, searing the morning air.
                             "Some of us
were soldiers," the buried whisper, "killed for country.
Still, war generates more war." "Where," Dust questions,
 "Where can we ever rest our crush of bones
and concrete, rise from our ruins as we cake
your grass and shake your headstones with our death?"

A graveyard facing the Hudson, among trees.
Behind the sheets rigged to the iron fence:
St. Paul's Chapel, where George and Martha Washington
knelt to pray. (The British — Cornwallis and Howe —
had occupied the pews and knelt there too.)

Handwriting clutches banners hugging the fence.
"We miss you!" "We remember you!" "God bless New York!"

How to reclaim that Nature in which Wordsworth
could hear "a still sad" human "music"
above the roar of bursting engines fueling
pyres of human flesh aflame? Reclaim
a land unpoisoned and unpoisonous,
Nobly conceived?
                       Pestled into the mortar
of its history, ash from past and present
cross its fields, blur into whirlwinds of its
willfulness, scattered farther, farther from
its heartland.
                     The last time I was here
I stood beside the iron fence, watched workmen
remove top layers of soil to be replaced
with fresh earth and new seeds. Would discards then
be sent to Fresh Kills Landfill's million-ton
debris from the blighted square? Sifted again,
perhaps, as if the ashes might pronounce
their names?

Wordsworth imaged a Hermit sitting alone
by the fire outside his Cave. I see a Country
sitting alone among nations, its eyes
made quiet, not by Harmony
but by a sense of power, itself a Nature
rampant, unconfined, the guide of its own
moral being, self-righteous, self-defined.

Yet there's another presence, interfused
With earth and ocean and the living air.
Call it a Unity of Being — a bond
the poet and the mystic apprehend.
Our dust, our ashes, day and night, the stars,
joy, horror, every foreign tongue —
all grope toward roots that mingle in the dark
while reaching for the light of common life.

Niagara Falls, after Ground Zero

Thundering past green islands
a hundred fifty feet
into the gorge,
river runs
over hard dolomite limestone
and layers of dolomite and shale,
runs as it has run for 12,000 years,
erodes one foot every decade
electrifies the riverbanks
and plunges toward
transfiguration.

People tested
their mettle by your danger.
Sam Patch jumped twice from Goat Island
and survived to die at Genesee Falls.
Annie Telson Taylor, a woman,
was first to go over in a barrel.
Blondin walked a tightrope across.

In 1874, an old schooner,
equipped with three bears and a buffalo,
two foxes and a raccoon,
a dog, a cat, and four geese,
was sent into the current as a stunt.
After the first rapids, two bears
were shot fleeing into Canada.
Terrified animals raced around the deck
spinning over the Falls.
Two geese survived.

White mist rises from you:
hallowed by rainbow,
an ark to Heaven.

On Goat Island,
below the spray
I close my eyes,
try to absorb the falling and rising
into my skin,
into my spirit
where the smoke of Ground Zero
hovers and whispers,
hovers and whispers
in rhythms of blood
meeting
the healing mist
of Nature,
and the permanent witness
of stars.

PROSPECT

> *. . . and suddenly, singly,*
> *mirrors which scoop again their outpoured beauty*
> *back into their own faces.*
>
> THE SECOND ELEGY

> *. . . and these things that live,*
> *slipping away, understand that you praise them;*
> *transitory themselves, they trust us for rescue,*
> *us, the most transient of all. They wish us to transmute them*
> *in our invisible heart—oh, infinitely into us!*
> *Whoever we are.*
>
> *Earth, isn't this what you want:* invisibly
> *to arise in us?*
>
> —Rainer Maria Rilke, THE NINTH ELEGY, "Duino Elegies"

As if the bridges, islands could be lifted
by angels — steel, the concrete, stones and bricks,
the people in their speed and sorrows — into
a band of sunlight — cars and windows, each
revolving door, the trash and treasure, hope,
the Bibles, Torahs, Qur'ans, Buddhist scripts,
a thousand sacred texts, discarded with
computers and their screens gone blank above
a gutted theater, whose bare-gummed stage
faces the orchestra with seats ripped out
like a toothless mouth, while aged men in boats
lie still below a bridge. Lift them, lift
the young men and the girls who stare out windows
like blank-eyed caryatids in a building
whose highest floors are empty, tenanted
by angels sometimes seen with folded wings
as they lie asleep on carpets.
                                        Then descend

to the street, go down three levels of subway, down
by escalator through those ghostly spaces
clutching at dust of vanished streets and shops,
the ragged sounds of wheels on cobblestones,
the trolleys, milkmen, each remembered face,
drums of every parade and public grief,
keep treading into the chambers of the heart.

Keep moving. Rise, go out and up the street
to rooms with rows of empty lockers, names
in chalk to be erased at will or whim,
an island of standing coffins on a feathered
floor, where phantom birds abide, alongside
parakeets in cages that survey
the Public Library and people reading.
Lift the dreaming floors with all their books,
call numbers, references, the language-pillars
of the world. Lift them to sky, another planet,
to begin again. Lift the forgiven past,
the judging present, future inspecting it,
funneled into ears as memorabilia
no one recalls yet holds aloft as trophy,
like the sound of a whirring rattle on New Year's Eve.

Cobbling out of thrum and clatter, yammer
of machines and people blasting rock to quarry
something durable and prime, we meant
to take some wisdom with us and denote
that we were here, we suffered, we endured,
and that we tilled a little while this tall
and tiny city, wounded at the tip,
and posed a wonder among exploding stars.

D. H. MELHEM, Ph.D., is the author of seven books of poetry, including *Country,* a book-length poem sequence about the United States, *Rest in Love,* a widely acclaimed elegy for her mother, and *Conversation with a Stonemason,* her most recent collection. Born in Brooklyn, New York, to Lebanese immigrants, a lifelong resident of New York City where her two children were born and raised, she has also published a novel, *Blight* (distributed by Syracuse University Press); two scholarly works, the first comprehensive study of Gwendolyn Brooks and an introduction to six Black poets (both from the University Press of Kentucky); a musical drama based on her poems about the West Side of Manhattan; over 60 essays; and two edited anthologies. Her *Notes on 94th Street* was the first poetry book in English by an Arab American woman and was proposed by Gwendolyn Brooks for a Pulitzer Prize nomination. Among Melhem's numerous awards for poetry and prose are a National Endowment for the Humanities Fellowship and an American Book Award for *Heroism in the New Black Poetry.* A Phi Beta Kappa graduate of New York University, in 2001 she received a Ph.D. Alumni Association Special Achievement Award from the City University of New York. She serves as vice-president of the International Women's Writing Guild. (Web site: dhmelhem.com)